FAMILY

REMINISCENCES

BY
LeGRAND M. JONES,
Of Trenton, Tenn.

ST. LOUIS:
C. R. BARNS PUBLISHING CO.,
1894.

PREFACE.

My son Silas some years ago requested me
to write a sketch of our family, before the facts
known to me should pass away with me and
be forgotten. I at first thought of confining
myself almost exclusively to genealogy; but I
have departed from this idea to some extent,
as will be seen. I have said little, if anything,
of the living, or of those facts known to my
children, or as accessible to them as to me. I
have, since my health gave way, frequently
regretted that I did not, during the lives of my
mother and my maternal grandmother, write
out and preserve the more prominent facts of
our family history, especially those relating to
our Huguenot ancestry. I could forty years
ago, no doubt, have carried the history of my
wife's family back a generation or two further.
I could probably have learned from Col. Woods
when his great-grandfather Woods came from
Ireland to North Carolina; and also, from my

wife's maternal grandfather, when his ancestors came to this country. But forty years ago I did not feel any particular interest in collecting and preserving these facts for my children. My wife had the family Bible, in which the record of her father's family was kept. When she got the Bible, after her father's death, it had gone pretty much to pieces. There is an impression in the family that, some years before her death, she took out the leaves containing this record, and gave them to her brother Levi for safe-keeping. Levi, I understand, is of the same impression ; but, if the record was placed in his hands, he has mislaid it. My sister gave our own family record, some years ago, to her brother Isaac, but he seems to have mislaid it. This will account for the omission of some dates as to births and deaths, that would otherwise be expected.

Most of the time I have been unable to write, and when able to do so, could write only a little at a time.

L. M. JONES.

TRENTON, Tenn., 1891.

FAMILY REMINISCENCES.

THE writer of the following paper was born in
Halifax County, Virginia, September 26th, 1817.
My father's name was James B. Jones, and my mother's maiden name was Elizabeth G. Cardwell. She
was the daughter of Mary Cardwell, who was the
daughter of Jeffrey Palmer. My maternal grandmother, Mary Palmer, first married a Cardwell. The
offspring of this union were three daughters, Susan
P., my mother, and Obedience T. Susan P., the oldest of the daughters, married Thomas O'Conner; and
Obedience, the youngest, married William Wilson.
After the death of Cardwell my grandmother married
a man by the name of Wray. Cardwell died before I
was born. I several times saw Wray when I was a
boy. He and Grandmother Wray were once at my
father's. I distinctly recollect that he was quite a
fleshy man. Moses and Labon P. Wray were the
only children of this marriage. After my grandmother married Wray, they lived in North Carolina
until the death of Mr. Wray. I am under the impression that Mr. Wray was a citizen of North
Carolina when he married my grandmother. After
the death of Mr. Wray, his widow with her two sons,
Moses and Labon, moved back to Halifax County,

Virginia, and lived with Uncle O'Conner. As stated, her oldest daughter had married Mr. O'Conner. My understanding is that Mr. Wray was a widower when he married my grandmother, and had one or more children living by a former wife; one of whom, a daughter, married Mead Wilson, a brother of the Wilson that married my aunt, Obedience T. My aunt was always called "Biddy" in the family.

William Wilson moved from North Carolina to Henry County, Tennessee, some years before my father left Virginia for Tennessee. Some two or three years after my father settled in Carroll County, Wilson also moved to Carroll County.

My great-grandfather, Jeffrey Palmer, lived near Hunting Creek Baptist Church, in Halifax County, Virginia. He died after I was born, but I was too young to remember him. He had five sons, Daniel, Jeffrey, Moses, Labon and Henry Palmer. Henry was the youngest of the sons. I do not know that I am giving their names in order. Henry had three daughters. One married a man named Trainham; Mary, my grandmother, first married a Cardwell; and one married a man named Threat—I believe that was his name, though I am not positive. They lived in Pittsylvania County, Virginia. I saw her but once. I was then quite a boy. Labon Palmer had but one child, a daughter, who married a Mr. Boyd. I recollect to have seen Boyd and his wife when I was a boy fifteen or sixteen years of age. They were at

Uncle O'Conner's who lived near Halifax Court House. I had gone there to attend a camp-meeting, and it seems that they were there for the same purpose. Mrs. Boyd was a very handsome lady. Boyd and wife paid a visit to this country some years before I was married. They were at Aunt O'Conner's and Mother's, but I did not see them.

I several times, when a boy, visited Halifax; and I knew all my mother's uncles, save Labon Palmer. I don't think I ever saw him. I am under the impression that he lived in Pittsylvania County.

Daniel Palmer was the man of whom my children have heard me speak as saying he "would never take another drink between Toot's Branch and Bannister's, unless he felt like it." Halifax Court House is situated between Toot's Branch and Bannister River. Uncle Daniel and some of the neighbors, as I heard the story, had been to the Court House one day, and while there Uncle Daniel had taken a few drinks too many, and was several sheets in the wind. Returning home, he got a ducking in Bannister River, and, as he thought, was in danger of being drowned. As he got out of the river, on the impulse of the moment, he exclaimed: "I will never take another drink between Toot's Branch and Bannister's!" Getting over his fright, and finding his money safe, after a long pause, he added, "unless I feel like it." I expect he was always true to this promise.

Jeffrey Palmer, the grandfather of my mother, was

a man of good property—might, I suppose, be said to have been wealthy.

Henry, the youngest of the boys, married Hannah, a daughter of my great-uncle, Elias Palmer. After his death, which was eight or ten years after my father came to this section, his widow and some of her children moved to and settled in Dyer County, Tennessee. Dr. Palmer was one of her children. Her daughter Susan married A. H. Smith, of McLemoresville.

A year or two after I was married, Aunt Hannah visited Mother. She and Mother came to Huntington and stayed with us several days. Aunt Hannah looked quite natural. I could see no change in her, from the time I had last seen her, when a boy, except that she looked slightly older. Mr. Smith and Cousin Susan, returning from a visit to Dyer, after they were married, called and stayed all night with us. I spent a delightful time in talking to her about "Old Virginia," and the persons we had known.

Uncle Jeffrey Palmer, my great-uncle, had a daughter named Susan. She married a man named Coats. He moved to Hardeman County shortly after my father came to Tennessee. In passing, he called on us; but for a great many years I have not heard from him or his family.

When Aunt Hannah moved to this county, she left a colored man behind. The owner of his wife did not wish to part with her, and perhaps his wife preferred

to remain. After his wife's death he came to this
country, and stayed several weeks at Mother's. He
had belonged to her grandfather, Jeffrey Palmer.
Mother had been raised on the plantation with him.
She was very glad to meet with him. I went to see
Mother while he was there. She had him called in
after supper, gave him a seat, and we had a long talk
with him about "old times," and his old master, Jeffrey Palmer, in particular.

The Lights, of Dyer County, are related to the
Palmers. Their mother was a sister of Aunt Hannah
Palmer and a daughter of old Uncle Elias Palmer.

I know but little about the other descendants of
Great-Grandfather Jeffrey Palmer. We kept up no
correspondence with them after we came to Tennessee. Indeed, I was never thrown much with my
mother's relations. When I was a boy my father
lived in Charlotte, and they in Halifax County. I
was taken by my mother, when she visited them, and
a few times visited Uncle O'Conner's family.

Jeffrey Palmer, my great-grandfather, ante-dated
the Revolutionary War. I think he was not a soldier
in the war, but hired a substitute.

On the maternal side my ancestors were of Huguenot descent. During the persecution of the Huguenots under Louis XIV of France, many of them fled
from that country to neighboring States. This was
especially the case after the repeal of the Edict of
Nantes, in 1685. Many of the Huguenots came to

South Carolina, and some to other States, North Carolina and Virginia. These kept up correspondence among themselves and relatives, and occasionally visited each other; so I learned from my mother. My recollection is that it was my great-grandmother Palmer's grandparents that were among the fugitives.*

I heard my mother and grandmother Wray frequently speak of the Huguenots, their mode of dress, etc. The older parties dressed pretty grandly, after the French style. I have heard my mother speak of the fact that while in France their Huguenot ancestors had a Bible. It was kept in a large, heavy chair, with a spring bottom, or with the bottom fastened down by a spring. Flax threads were wound through all the leaves, passing over the back of the book, where they were fastened together, for its better preservation. When the Bible was read they always kept some one on the watch, to prevent surprise. After reading, it was carefully placed away in the chair, and the bottom fastened with the spring. The chair was so constructed that you could handle it and never suspect that anything was in it, or that it was anything more than a large framed chair.

My mother said that her grandmother Palmer was one of the most elegant and quiet ladies she ever knew.

---

* Since this was written, I have received a letter from one of the family relatives, who states that my memory is correct as to this fact.

She said she never saw her give way to ill-temper or anger in her life, or do anything unbecoming a lady. Her grandfather was a most excellent man, honorable in all the walks of life, but quick-tempered. In this latter respect he and his wife differed.

I have, since my health gave way, frequently regretted that I had not taken more interest in this part of the family history, and learned from my mother, Grandmother Ray and Aunt O'Conner, fuller particulars of our Huguenot progenitors. They knew the Huguenot families that first came to this country, and could have given many interesting family incidents connected with them. As stated, it was my great-grandmother Palmer's grandparents that were among the fugitives. My name, "LeGrand Michaux," is French; and this is the way we have the family name. I do not know from what country the Palmers emigrated.

Uncle O'Conner died during the first year after my father came to Tennessee.

In the fall of 1836 my father went back to Virginia to close up his business, and Aunt O'Conner, her family, Grandmother Wray and her two sons, Moses and Labon, came back with him. After Grandmother Wray was married the second time, she and her husband went to North Carolina, taking with them her youngest daughter, Obedience. My mother remained with her grandparents until she was married.

Labon Wray, two or three years after coming to

Tennessee, married a Miss Hall, niece of Rev. James and Robert Hurt. Wray died a few days after my return from Mexico, in the spring of 1847.

Moses Wray married a lady in Weakley County, and died a few years after his brother Labon.

Grandmother Wray lived with Aunt O'Conner, and died at an advanced age. She was over eighty years when she died. I have remarked that Aunt Hannah Palmer married Henry Palmer, her cousin, son of Jeffrey Palmer, my mother's grandfather. Hannah Palmer was the daughter of Elias Palmer, brother of Jeffrey Palmer, the elder.

Elias Palmer lived on the Coles' Ferry Road, near where the Morton's Ferry Road leaves that road. When a boy, I went with my mother several times to visit her relatives in Halifax, and I was with her during those visits at his house. He was quite an old man, and may have appeared older than he really was. I understood that he was a soldier in the Revolutionary War. I have heard my mother speak of the fact that he said the sweetest bread he ever ate he made up on his handkerchief and bak´d in the ashes. He and his command had been running from the British. They at the time had nothing but a little corn-meal to eat. Reaching a spring where a halt was ordered, they got water, and he made up his ration of meal, baked and ate, as stated. The old gentleman was always fond of taking his peach brandy and honey before breakfast. This was a very common practice in his day.

My mother had a great uncle named LeGrand, who was mortally wounded by a round shot or bomb in some battle in South Carolina. She several times showed me a buckle he was wearing at the time. It may have been a knee-buckle. It has the appearance of having been battered in some way. I suppose my sister Bettie Ann has it yet. Mother stated how it was brought from South Carolina to Halifax, but I have forgotten. It was sent as a memento.

On one of Mother's visits to Halifax, she took Pleasant, a colored boy, with her as a nurse. Pleasant and myself are about the same age. When she got to Uncle O'Conner's, Mother said to Pleasant, "If you go through that gate," meaning the yard gate, "I will whip you." Uncle O'Conner was a wheelwright, and employed a good many hands in making wagons, etc. She was afraid to have Pleasant take the child out to the shops, where the hands were engaged at work. She had not been at Uncle O'Conner's long before Pleasant and the child were missing. Mother called him up, and was about to let in on him, saying, "Didn't I tell you that if you went through that gate I would whip you?" He at once answered: "Lord, Mistiss, I didn't go through the gate; I got over the fence!" This ended the matter. I never heard a better piece of special pleading than this. Pleasant is now living in Carroll County, and doing well.

William Jones was the name of my paternal grandfather. He also lived in Halifax County, not more than two or three miles from where old Uncle Elias Palmer lived. I was frequently at his house, when a boy. He died several years before my father came to Tennessee. He was quite an old man at my earliest recollection. For a year or two before he died he was somewhat paralyzed. I recollect being at his house one time when he walked very badly, and had to hold to something to enable him to walk or stand. His wife was a Miss Brown. She was called Patsy. In my earlier years I understood that my grandfather Jones served a short time in the Revolutionary War.

Two or three years after my father left Virginia, Grandmother Jones and her family also came to Tennessee. Her son, Uncle William Jones, and family, R. Wyatt and family (Wyatt had married her daughter Sarah), her daughters Jane and Betsy, came with her. These daughters were not married. Aunt Jane became paralyzed, and died at my mother's during the latter part of the war. My grandmother Jones lived to be very old, nearly one hundred years. I do not recollect the year of her death. After ninety years of age she was able to walk about the neighborhood. Her memory had suffered but little from old age. If she had a defective tooth in her head I do not know it. She was stoutly built, but not over medium height.

My great-grandfather Jones' name was Robert, as I

learned. I am not able to trace the paternal line
beyond my grandfather, William Jones. I do not
know in what year his family came to this country.
I have always understood they were of Welsh descent.

My son Silas will recollect Cousin Ryal Bryant,
who lived near Shady Grove, and who died a few
years after the war.

I have stated that in the maternal line our ancestry
were French Huguenots, and that many Huguenots
fled from France and settled in South Carolina during
the reign of Louis XIV. Soon after coming to Tennessee, my father and Mr. Bryant became acquainted.
Bryant had moved from South Carolina some years
before my father came to this section, and was living
in Shady Grove, in Gibson County. After becoming
acquainted it was ascertained that his wife and my
mother were related. Both families belonged to the
old Huguenot stock. My mother and his wife, so I
learned, were able to trace the relationship. It was
remote, however; perhaps not nearer than third or
fourth cousin; and hence, in speaking to or of each
other, I always said "Cousin Ryal," and he, "Cousin
LeGrand "

Col. Jackson's wife, Zack's mother, was of the same
stock, as I understand. I rather think that she and
Bryant's wife were sisters; am not certain; but this
can be easily ascertained. I was frequently at Cousin
Ryal Bryant's house, but only slightly acquainted
with Col. Jackson. Zack Jackson was the only mem-

ber of the family with whom I was much acquainted.
I am not certain but that my father and Cousin Ryal
were also remotely related.

My father's people were Baptists. I do not know
that my great-grandfather Palmer or his sons were
church-members, but I infer that they were Baptist
in sentiment. When I was a boy there were few
Methodists and no Cumberlands in the section of
Virginia in which we lived. The Baptist was the
leading denomination, the Presbyterian next, and
then the Episcopalian.

My father moved from Halifax County to Charlotte
County when I was in my second year; and lived as
overseer on a plantation belonging to Letsy Carrington. This plantation was situated on the Roanoke, a
small stream, near where it flowed into Stanton River.
At this place my brother Silas was born. Father
lived here for two or three years, and then for six
years lived as overseer on a plantation owned by
Paul Carrington. This plantation lay twelve or fifteen miles higher up Stanton River. No white family
lived on either place at the time, save my father's.
It was while Father lived at this place that Silas and
I first went to school. I was not more than seven
years old, and Silas about eighteen months younger.
The school was taught in the Baptist church near
Coles' Ferry. The house was a log building. It was
taken down a year or two after this, and a frame
building put up in its place. It was about four miles

from where my father lived: a pretty long walk for
two little boys. In bad weather we were generally
taken to school, and frequently some one would meet
us in the evening. Our teacher was a young man
from the North. His name was Hawley. Under him
I first studied grammar; Murray's was the one used.
It was a large work and unsuited to beginners. I
committed the rules to memory, and could repeat
them pretty well. I will for the benefit of my grandchildren give the rules or definitions for the noun and
verb:

"A substantive or noun is the name of anything
that exists, or of which we have any notion, as Lon-
don, man, virtue."

"A verb is a word which signifies to be, to do, or
to suffer, as, I am, I rule, I am ruled."

I had no conception of the meaning of these rules
at the time. My teacher never explained them to me.
Had he done so I would readily have understood
their meaning. I have never had much respect for
his memory. I have taught school myself, and never
had any trouble in making children understand
"noun," "verb" and "adjective;" indeed, the leading
parts of speech.

My father next lived with Mrs. Carrington, the
mother of Paul Carrington, for five years. She and
her family lived on a plantation lying on Roanoke and
Twitty's Creek, three or four miles above the one first-
mentioned. There were many such plantations in

this part of Virginia at the time of which I am speaking. Many of the owners lived in baronial style.

John Randolph's residence was three miles up Stanton River from the Letsy Carrington place. He owned several other plantations in Charlotte County. The wealth, culture, refinement and hospitality of Virginia were found in these homes. When Randolph rode out from home he went in his coach drawn by four horses, and attended by two servants. He was a real aristocrat, and in many respects a remarkable man. As an orator he was never excelled by any in his State, except Patrick Henry.

There is now a railroad which runs down Twitty's Creek and crosses Stanton River some short distance above where the Roanoke empties into it.

I have some slight recollection of a few things that occurred while my father lived at the place first mentioned. I remember some ladies visiting my mother at one time, and also of pulling or rolling up my pants and wading in a pond of water. Of course I got a scolding for it. I think an old mare or horse got after me one day and scared me pretty badly.

My recollection is tolerably distinct after my father moved to the place belonging to Paul Carrington. It was the first year that my father lived at this place that a mare kicked me and broke my leg. I had seen my father and some of the negro men milk her. She may have lost her colt, as a reason for this. My father and a negro man were standing around her

one day, and I thought I would milk her too. She
kicked me and broke my left leg between the hip joint
and knee. My father carried me into the house, laid
me on a bed, and examined my leg to see if it was
broken. He sent for a doctor. My leg was set and
bandaged; a nice little box was made, a part of which
ran up under my left arm; my leg was placed and
confined in it by passing cords over the box, and in
this way I lay on my back for a number of weeks.
This same mare ran away with me a few years after
this time. My father, mother and the children had
attended a Fourth of July celebration. We crossed
Stanton River at Coles Ferry; the celebration was
just on the opposite side of the river from the Ferry.
My father was on horseback and I was on the grey
mare. Mother, the other children, and, I think,
some ladies were in the carryall. In returning, after
crossing the river, (there were a number of persons
in company), I was riding behind the carryall with my
father and some others. A light shower of rain came
up; the mare became restless, and I became alarmed.
I was only about ten years old. She dashed by the
carryall and ran through some small timber. I held
my head down to keep from being knocked off by the
limbs. The mare put out for home as hard as she
could clatter. I knew that about a mile ahead of us
there was a long hill to descend, and I was afraid that
in going down this hill I would either fall off or be
thrown over her head and killed. Just before reach-

ing the hill, the road, as I knew, passed over a level, sandy piece of ground. I made up my mind to jump off when I reached this place in the road. I picked my place on reaching the sandy part of the road, and threw myself off, trying to catch on my feet, but found myself on my back. I knew Mother was alarmed, and that some one would follow on to see what had become of me. So I sprang upon my feet. In a moment or two some one came in sight, and seeing me standing, turned back to let Mother know I was safe.

In the fall of 1832 my father rented a place of a man named Barkesdale, lying on Stanton River, six or seven miles west of Watkins' Store, and lived there until 1833. He then rented a plantation from Mrs. Read, lying on Twitty's Creek, two or three miles east of Watkins' Store.

In the fall of 1833, while my father was living at the Barkesdale place, the wonderful meteoric shower occurred, about which much has been written. Brother Silas and I were sleeping up stairs. About day, or perhaps a little before, Charles (a colored man) came running to the house, crying out in great alarm, "Master! Master! the stars are falling!" This awoke Silas and myself, and we came down stairs. The heavens were ablaze with what seemed to be falling stars. It was a grand, a wonderful and an awful sight. The explosive and whizzing sounds of the meteors were continually heard. Long streams of fiery light remained in the track of many of them. The meteoric shower continued until obscured by the morning light. The whizzing sound of the meteors, though somewhat abated, could be heard for some time after it was too light to see them. Father and Mother looked serious, but not alarmed, and hence I was not frightened. Many thought that the last day had come, and hence were much alarmed. Charles at this time was not a professor of religion.

My father was a deacon of the Baptist Church from my earliest recollection. His membership was first with a church not far from Coles' Ferry; the same building at which the school was taught, of which I have spoken. When he moved to Mrs. Carrington's, he joined the Baptist church near Watkins' Store, called Mossingford. His membership remained with this church until he left Virginia for Tennessee.

ABNER W. CLOPTON was the leading Baptist minister in that part of Virginia in which my father lived. He was the first preacher of any denomination that I recollect having seen or heard. He was an educated man—I think a graduate of Chapel Hill, North Carolina. He was greatly respected by all classes and denominations, and beloved by the members of his churches. He was eminently useful. He was conservative and liberal in his views, and preached Baptist doctrines in charity to all other denominations. From my earliest recollection until his death, he was fre-

quently at my father's house, and I knew him better
than any other minister of the Gospel. His demeanor
was marked by gravity, and, as I thought, shaded at
times by an expression of sadness. His churches all
prospered under his ministry. I have heard my father
remark that he knew men who were more gifted in the
pulpit, but as a pastor, and for influence in the community, he knew no man who was his equal. When I
was a small boy he introduced Sabbath-schools in his
churches. I think he was the first to introduce them
in that part of the State. In connection with Sunday-
schools he organized Bible classes for the purpose of
studying the Scriptures. There was a class of this
kind in the Baptist church near Coles' Ferry. A
year or two after this class was organized, I heard
my father and mother speak of the fact that, with
one or two exceptions, the young men who were members of the class had all professed religion. He also
at an early day introduced temperance societies in
the community in which he lived. I and my brother
Silas, though small boys, joined the society. The
members were pledged against the use of all intoxicating liquors, except when necessary as a medicine.
I have at all times kept pretty close to this pledge.
My father at first did not join. He said he was getting old and did not expect it would be a benefit to
him; but was heartily in favor of the young becoming
members, to whom the pledge would most probably
be beneficial. But it was not long before he changed

his mind and joined; giving as his reason that his example should be on the right side. I can remember when my father was in the habit of taking his daily dram; but after he became a member of the society I never knew of his touching a drop, and he was ever afterwards a decided advocate of abstinence from all intoxicating drinks.

Elder Clopton impressed upon the members of his churches, who were heads of families, the importance of holding family worship. He attached great importance to the early and proper training of children. He wished to see the family altar set up in every house. It was under his influence that my father began having family prayers. I remember the first night that Father held prayers in his family. I suppose I was at the time about twelve years old. The fifty-first division of the Psalms was read upon that occasion. After this my father kept up family worship during his life. Elder Clopton conducted protracted meetings very much as my children have seen Brother Hillsman conduct such meetings. The anxious were invited to the front seat, and the church would join with and for them in prayer. He frequently, at the regular meetings, gave the invitation, if any present desired the prayers of the church, for them to come forward, and the church would join in prayer for them.

It was during a protracted meeting at Mossingford that my brother Silas professed religion. He was

then about eleven years old. He joined the church
and was baptized by Brother Clopton, who had also
baptized my mother.

Elder Clopton was active in the cause of missions.
He taught the members of his church that it was a
duty enjoined by the Scriptures to aid in preaching
the Gospel to every creature. Some of those members have emigrated to the Tennessee country; and
whenever you meet with one of them it is not difficult
to get him to cast in his mite to help send the word of
life to the heathen.

He generally had one or more young men with him
whom he was training for the ministry. I remember
James McAlister and Isaac S. Tinsly. McAlister, I
think, was consumptive, and died young. Tinsley's
name appears as a delegate to the convention, in 1811,
that organized the Southern Baptist Convention.

I have stated that Clopton preached the distinctive
doctrines of the Baptists plainly and clearly, when he
thought the occasion required; but he was careful to
give no unnecessary offense to other denominations.
He had one Sabbath morning baptized a large number
of persons at Mossingford, and before administering
the ordinance gave the reason why Baptists practice
immersion. On returning to the church, Tinsly took
as his text the 19th and 20th verses of the 28th chapter of Matthew, and preached a sermon upon the
subject of Baptism, antagonizing the practice of other
denominations. After we had returned from church,

I heard Father and Mother conversing about the sermon Tinsly had preached. Father said that after the congregation was dismissed Brother Clopton had a conversation with him, in which he said: "I thought I said all that was necessary on the subject at the water. I did not know that Tinsly intended preaching such a sermon. I thought his discussion was ill-timed." He thought Tinsly should have advised with him before preaching such a sermon. My father entirely agreed with him. A good many Presbyterians had attended the Baptist church that day; none of them were brought over to Baptist views, and the Baptists were already strong enough in the faith.

My brother Clopton, who was mortally wounded at the battle of Stone's River, near Murfreesborough, was named for Elder Clopton.

The Baptist house for worship at Mossingford was a large frame building, with a long wing at the left of the pulpit for the colored people, separated by a low railing from that portion of the building occupied by the whites. The church had a large colored membership. Many of John Randolph's negroes belonged to this church. Randolph had a colored man named Phil. Elder Clopton and my father had great respect for Phil, as a worthy, upright Christian. When any of Randolph's negroes proposed joining the church, my father always consulted with Phil as to their Christian character. Phil's opinion was generally, if not invariably, accepted and followed by the church.

Services were held monthly on Saturday and Sunday; and many of the colored people were permitted to attend church on Saturday. The Sacrament was administered to the white and colored people at the same time, the colored members remaining in that portion of the building allotted to them. On these occasions my father or some one of the deacons would hand the bread and wine to the colored deacons, and they would pass them around to the colored members, while the white deacons waited on the white members. I recollect on one occasion, when there was a large congregation in attendance, some white men, not knowing the rules of the church, took seats in that portion of the church set apart for the colored people. My father quietly stepped up to them and told them their mistake. They understood, and in a very orderly manner left the seats they had taken.

DANIEL WITT.—I remember Witt very well. He was frequently at my father's house when I was a boy. He was then a young man. He was well set; a little below medium height. There was a good deal of suavity in his composition. He was very agreeable and pleasant in the social circle, and attractive as a preacher. His style was never studied, but easy and fluent; he never hesitated for a word. At times he became animated, but never impassioned. He never tired his congregation, but left his hearers feeling they wished he had preached a little longer. This is the impression I have retained of him from my boyhood. I do not remember his being at my father's house, or seeing him, for several years before my father left Virginia. I suppose he was occupying some other field of labor.

J. B. JETER.—I saw him several times at Mossing-ford. I remember something of his personal appearance; he was tall and spare. But I have retained no impression whatever of his style of preaching. He was also a young man at the time; he had not been preaching long. I had seen and heard Witt before I saw Jeter.

ELDER JOHN WEATHERFORD.—My father and mother both knew Elder Weatherford before they were married, and had frequently heard him preach. I have heard my mother speak of his being at her grandfather Palmer's when she was a girl.

Weatherford, before the Revolutionary War, had been imprisoned in Chesterfield jail for preaching. In my boyish days I thought it very strange that any one had ever been imprisoned, in this country, for preaching. I desired very much to see a man who had been imprisoned on this account. While imprisoned, people frequently gathered around the jail, and Weatherford would preach to them from the jail windows. To prevent this, a wall or some obstruction was built in front of the windows; but, not to be out-done, people would frequently gather around the wall, and upon some signal he would preach to them. It was stated that, as a signal, a handkerchief would be hoisted upon a staff or pole.

About 1830 or 1831, Elder Weatherford visited many of the churches to which he had preached in his earlier days. While on this round, he came to Mossingford and was present on Saturday and Sunday, the regular days for worship. He preached on Sunday. He was then very old; I believe it was said he was something over ninety years at the time. His appearance indicated great age. His feeble condition was very apparent. He was tall and inclined to be raw-boned. He wore a knit woolen cap on his head all the time. In my later years, though I thought nothing of it at the time, I could look back and see that he was a man of marked character; that he was a man among men, cut out for a leader.

There was a seat prepared for him in front of the pulpit. My father took me and my next oldest brother, presented us to him, and he took our hands in his. All, or nearly all, the older people shook hands with him as they came in the church. Some of them seemed very much affected at meeting with him. To many of them he had some remark to make. His text on Sunday was Luke ii : 10-11 " Behold, I bring you good tidings," etc. Elder Clopton read the text at Weatherford's request. I think he could not see well enough to read; but he could talk. At times he became animated, and was highly interested in his subject. Judging from what I recollect of his manner on the occasion, he must, when in the vigor of manhood, have preached with no ordinary power and effect. As he closed his sermon, he remarked that the Gospel he had that day attempted to preach was the same he had preached to listening crowds from the windows of Chesterfield jail. It was the only allusion he made to his imprisonment. Before he closed his sermon, my father went up into the pulpit, stood by his side and held him up. His wife, who was sitting near my father, requested him, as I afterwards learned, to go and stand by him, for fear of his falling. At the conclusion of his sermon, Elder Clopton said to the congregation that the older citizens all knew the character and circumstances of the old brother. If any of them wished to contribute anything to him and his wife, they could do so as they left the church. It seemed to me that almost everybody wished to give them something. Indeed, during his tour the people everywhere, as I learned, showed their regard for him by liberal contributions. I think his home at that time was in Pittsylvania County.

This tour of Elder Weatherford brought up the subject of his imprisonment and release, and I heard it talked of by Father and others. It was the received opinion of that day that he was released through the instrumentality of Patrick Henry. Just how this was effected I do not know. Mr. Henry was regarded, in the part of Virginia in which my father lived, as the great pioneer of religious liberty. In his speeches and public utterances upon this subject, tradition said he was bold and outspoken.

My father and the men of his day were in their earlier years acquainted with many persons who antedated the Revolutionary War, and who were co-temporary with Mr. Henry and Elder Weatherford; and I do not well see how they could be mistaken as to these important facts. The fact of Weatherford's imprisonment would especially have attracted the attention of Baptists at the time. It was a matter in which they were deeply interested. They could but have felt they were persecuted in the person of their leader; and it would naturally have been a matter of frequent conversation when they met. His release, and by whose instrumentality, would have been a matter of equal interest; and hence I cannot see how they could have been mistaken, or the traditions of the time erroneous. Others may speak disparagingly of the part Mr. Henry took in the cause of religious liberty, and the protection he gave Baptists; but surely *Baptists* should never do this.

That Mr. Henry looked to the entire separation of Church and State, when he became the advocate of religious liberty, is more than I can say. How this was I do not know. But it is easy to see that, the first great step taken, the others would necessarily follow.

The part borne by Mr. Jefferson, Mr. Madison and others in this cause, at a later day, was more a matter of record and of written history at the time, and hence has been better preserved. That borne by Mr. Henry was mainly in speeches and public utterances. It was in this way that he gave an impetus to the cause of religious liberty.* But these utterances not being reduced to writing at the time, his work soon came to rest mainly in tradition, liable to pass away and be forgotten.

JOHN KEER.—In the fall of 1833 I attended a meeting at Wynn's Creek Camp Ground, Halifax County. It was there that I heard and saw John Keer. In person he was noble and commanding. His voice was deep, full-toned and of great compass. There was a large congregation in attendance. The occasion was one to animate him and call forth his powers. His text was Ezekiel xxxiii:11. I have never heard such a sermon, or heard such a public speaker. I have seen no man in Church or State that possessed his powers as an orator. He possessed great power. Much of his sermon I remember to this day. There were no mere flights of the imagination no dealing in fancy work. His language was plain and simple, and every word seemed to be used to carry conviction to the minds of his hearers. With him words were things. You saw things as he saw them; you felt as he felt; your mind followed his mind; his convictions became your convictions. At one time he drew a picture of Satan with his black banner, his Satanic followers, and the dark and hideous crowd which followed that banner; and in immediate contrast he presented Christ with the banner of the Cross, all radiant with light and love and glory, and the happy and blessed throng of heaven and earth as his attendants. The choice between the two was demanded. The impulse seemed irresistible to burst away from Satan and his black and hideous followers, and fly to the banner of Christ and the Cross.

Elias Dodson, a name familiar to the Baptists of North Carolina and Virginia, was several times at my house some years after I came to Trenton. On one of these occasions I mentioned having heard Keer, and the impression he made upon me. Dodson had often heard him. He fully concurred in the opinion I had formed of him. As illustrative of his great power over his hearers, Dodson related an incident that occurred in some place where Keer was preaching. The place I have forgotten: A young man was ridiculing to his companions the idea that one could not sit unmoved under Keer's preaching. He said it was all weakness, and he would show them. "I will go and hear him, and you shall see that I will behave myself and not give way to any such weakness." The young man went, full of self conceit, and took a prominent seat in front of the stand. He was one of the first to surrender and cry out for mercy.

REMOVAL TO TENNESSEE.—My father left Virginia for West Tennessee in October, 1835. The weather was all that could be desired, and we had a very pleasant time on the road. Mother had been in bad health for some years, and it was thought she would have to stay in some house at night. But she stayed in the tent every night while travelling. Her health began to improve from the first, and continued to improve to the end of the journey. We had been on the road but a day or two, when we fell in company with Elder Elisha Collins, the grandfather of E. A. Collins of Milan, Tenn. The meeting, I think, was by previous arrangement. Elder Collins was moving out some negroes to Henderson County. His white family was not brought out until the next fall. We travelled in company until we passed Columbia, when Elder Collins kept the road to Henderson County. My father turned to the right, crossed the Tennessee River at Reynoldsburg, and came through Henry County to see Uncle Wilson's family. Elder Collins was a Baptist preacher. He was a well-informed man, and of decidedly more than average pulpit ability.

My father had accumulated a right handsome property, for the times, before leaving Virginia. His property consisted mainly in negroes. The first year after coming to Tennessee he rented a place from a man named David Marshall, lying about two miles south and west of McLemoresville. That summer he bought the land on the Paris Road, north and west of

McLemoresville, on which the family lived until Mr. Brower sold and moved to Trezevant, a few years ago.

My father was a soldier in the war of 1812. His command was in Washington soon after the British left that city. He went as far as Ellicott's Mills, in Maryland. He was a man of unblemished Christian character, respected and beloved in every community in which he lived. He was an active and leading member in his church. I have thought he lived as near the golden rule, " As ye would that men should do to you, do ye even so to them," as any man I ever saw.

My father died on the 9th of November, 1840. He was about fifty-five years of age. His end was entirely peaceful. Old Brother Baylor Walker talked with him on the subject of his hope a few days before he died. He had no fears of death. He expressed himself with great satisfaction as to his hope. I was present and heard the conversation. A few days before he had this conversation with Brother Walker, he made some remark which led me to believe he thought he would not get well. I said to him, " I do not think you are going to leave us, Father; but if you should, I will do the best I can for Mother and the children." These were the only words that ever passed between us on the subject. I have ever remembered them, and feel that I have been faithful to what I then said to him.

His estate was a good deal embarrassed when he died; and for several years the management of his affairs, in my efforts to save the property, cost me no little anxiety and many sleepless hours.

My father and mother had the following children: The writer, LeGrand Michaux, named for our Huguenot ancestors (I write the name in full for the benefit of my grandchildren); Silas P., born April 29th, 1819; Paul S., Moses A., Abraham C., Isaac W., James D., Bettie Anna, and a daughter named Mary, about a year old when we left Virginia. This daughter died soon after we came to this country. After coming to this country, Clopton and Doddridge were born; Clopton, the year after we came to Tennessee, while living on the Marshall place; Doddridge, after Father bought and settled on the place I have referred to. Bettie Ann was born March 20th, 1833. She married Mr. Thomas K. Brower, Nov. 19th, 1851.

Clopton and Doddridge both enlisted in the Confederate service. Doddridge was taken sick at Corinth, and carried to Memphis, where he was waited on by Paul and James until he died. James brought the body home in a metallic case. It was buried in the family burying ground.

Clopton was mortally wounded at the battle of Stone's River, near Murfreesborough. He lingered several days, and died. Mrs. Thomas Hutcherson, sister of John and Bennett Hillsman, saw him while in the hospital after he was wounded, and talked with

him. He sent word to Mother by Mrs. Hutcherson
that he was not afraid to die. He was well cared for
in the hospital until his death, as I learned. Some
of the children, after the war closed, wanted to bring
the body home and bury it in the family grave-yard,
but Mother opposed it, saying she could not bear it
Clopton and Doddridge were both professors of religion, and both members of the church at McLemoresville.

My daughter Clopton is named for her uncle Clopton, and my son Doddridge for his uncle Doddridge.

MY MOTHER.—My mother lived a widow for about
twenty-eight years. She was born the 28th of May,
1798, and died on the 30th of February, 1869. I
received a dispatch about the middle of the day that
she was seriously ill. I left my office, went out home;
and in a short time was on my way to see her. I got
to her house a little after dark. She lived five or six
days after I reached the old homestead. I remained
with her to the end, and saw her buried in the family
burying-ground. The burying-ground is a little north
of the house. My father selected this place, and was
the first to be buried in it. While Mother was sick
she saw all her children, save Abraham, who was in
Arkansas. Her end was entirely peaceful. I talked
with her on the subject. She told me all was well
with her. There were no clouds between her and the
better world.

My mother was greatly above the average woman.
She possessed large common sense, strong will, decis-
ion of character; and was eminently fitted to govern
a household. She united in a high degree business
qualities with refinement and delicacy of feeling. Her
strong will was tempered by good sense and a gentle
and loving nature. She was a fine housewife, an excellent economist, and was rarely, if ever, excelled in
those qualities of heart and mind that make the model
wife and mother.

MARCH, 1843, was a remarkable month. It was the
coldest month of the year. I never before saw, nor
since have seen, the weather in March anything like
so cold. There were several heavy snow storms during the time; and from early in the month up to about
the 24th the ponds and creeks were covered with ice
four or five inches thick. Fine ice was gathered on
the creek at Huntingdon and put up during this time.

The great comet of 1843 also made its appearance
during this month. It came from the west and passed
around the sun, going so near the sun that the nucleus
was not seen, at least not with the naked eye. The
tail was not seen until the comet had passed nearly
around the sun and was leaving the earth. When
first seen, it appeared in all its beauty and splendor.
To the eye, the tail appeared to extend half way up
the heavens. The concurrence of the comet and the
severe cold of March caused some to feel serious, im-

agining that the near proximity of the great comet was affecting our atmosphere.

STUDY OF THE LAW.—About a year after my father's death, I borrowed Blackstone's Commentaries of G. H. Raulston, of Huntingdon; studied law at home awhile; then went to Huntingdon and studied under Judge B. C. Totton. He was an older brother of Judge A. O. W. Totton. In April, 1843, I obtained license to practice law. My license was signed by Judge Totton and by Judge Reed, of Jackson, Tenn. I was then in my twenty-sixth year.

TRIP TO MEXICO.—In June, 1846, I started as a member of a volunteer company for the Mexican War. H. F. Murray was the Captain of this company. We landed on what was called Brazos Island about the first of July. After some delay at this place, we passed on up the Rio Grande, and made different encampments along the river. We were not organized into a regiment until some little time after we left Brazos Island. Four West Tennessee and four East Tennessee companies composed the regiment. W. T. Haskell was elected our Colonel, and he appointed me Sergeant Major. After the organization of the regiment we moved up the river to Camargo, a town on a stream that flows into the Rio Grande. Our camp was just above the town. Here the army corps to which we belonged remained until late in the fall;

when the march was taken up for Vera Cruz. While
at Camargo a great many of the men had diarrhea,
and here we lost several of our company. When the
regiment left I had been down with diarrhea for several weeks, unable to travel, and was left in the hospital. I remained at Camargo until the last days of
December, when the sick, or many of them, were
taken by boat to Matamoras. We were going down
the river on Christmas day. It was a beautiful day,
warm enough to go about without wearing a coat. I
remained in the hospital at Matamoras until early in
February, when I obtained a furlough for the purpose
of trying to get back home. When I got back to
Brazos Island, the place where we had debarked the
year before, I called on General Scott. When he saw
my condition, he gave me a discharge, telling me to
get home, that I would not be able to get back to
Mexico. While at Matamoras I was reduced almost
to a skeleton. There was one week of the time in
which I do not think I ate as much as a slice of light
bread or drank a cup of tea. I had to use beef tea.

N. B. Burrow, a brother of John J. Burrow, called
on me just before he left Matamoras for Vera Cruz. I
am sure he had no thought of my getting up again
when he left me. He seemed very reluctant to leave
me.

With the blessing of heaven, I reached New Or-
leans, and took a boat to Will's Point, Benton County.
Brother Paul met me at this place with a horse, and

so I got safely home. It was a year or two after I
returned before my health was fully restored.

MARRIAGE.—On the second of October, 1850, I
married Miss Cassandra Woods, daughter of Levi S.
and Aranthia J. Woods. Rev. James M. Hurt performed the ceremony.

MY WIFE'S MATERNAL ANCESTRY.—Mrs. Woods
was the daughter of James Dinwiddie, of Henry
County. His father was also named James. The
older or last-mentioned Dinwiddie emigrated from
Pennsylvania to Virginia at an early day, remained
there some years, and in the summer of 1787 moved to
and settled in Fayette County, Kentucky; whence, in
the summer of 1792, he moved to Madison County,
Kentucky. Mr. James Dinwiddie, my wife's grandfather, was born in Virginia, September 9th, 1782,
and died September 4th, 1860. He was twice married. His first wife was Cassandra Harris. She was
born September 18th, 1787, and they were married
February 23d, 1804. This marriage took place in
Kentucky. They had two children, James, and
Aranthia Jane, who married Levi S. Woods. Mrs.
Woods' brother, named for his father, married and
lived near Lavonia for a number of years. He was a
very intelligent man, of high moral worth. I was
well acquainted with him. He moved to Arkansas,
and lived but a few years after he left Tennessee. I

tried to dissuade him from going to Arkansas. He
had been in poor health for many years, and thought
the change would be beneficial to him.

Grandfather Dinwiddie's second wife was named
Mary Carson. She was born August 5th, 1786, and
died September 18th, 1878. This marriage took place
in Virginia, December 29th, 1814. Mr. Dinwiddie,
my wife's grandfather, moved to Carroll County, Tennessee, in 1823; and in the fall of that year moved to
Henry County, where he lived until his death.

The children of Mr. Dinwiddie by his second wife
were: Thomas H., Newton, William, Baker and Mary.

James Dinwiddie, my wife's great-grandfather,
moved to Henry County in 1824, where he lived until
his death. His wife's maiden name was Helm. I
have not been able to trace this branch of the family
further back.

The Dinwiddies were all Presbyterians, but after
the great revival that broke out in Kentucky about
1800, and which extended into Tennessee, they united
with the Cumberlands. I have at different times
heard old persons speak of this revival; have heard
Grandfather Dinwiddie speak of it. This revival, in
its character and circumstances, seems strange to us
of the present day. People were very eager to hear
the Gospel; they would go many miles to attend these
meetings. At the meetings many would be prostrat-
ed; some would be found lying on the ground in the
woods as if insensible, and would remain in this con-

dition for hours; and, when relieved from the conviction and burden of sin, would rise rejoicing, seemingly
from an unconscious state.

Mr. Dinwiddie was several times at my house after
I married his grand-daughter. I formed a very high
opinion of him. He was a man of vigorous common
sense, of noble impulses, a leader in his church and
community, and one of the best citizens of Henry
County. I formed the opinion that in temper he was
quick and impulsive, but incapable of meditating or
doing what he believed to be wrong. He was a very
successful.farmer, and accumulated a handsome estate. I learned from Cass that when he visited her
mother he would, before leaving, always call the family together and pray with and for them.

Mrs. Woods, my mother-in-law, died on the 28th of
March, 1853, aged forty-two years, five months and
two days; Col. Woods, on the 28th of November, 1857.
Both were buried in the burying-ground at the Presbyterian Church, on the old stage road leading from
Huntingdon to Jackson, of which church they were
members. Col. and Mrs. Woods had the following
children : Nancy, who married James M. Lanier, several years before I was married ; Cassandra Charity
Harris, my wife; William; James; Mary; John
(always called Jack); Andrew; Georgia and Levi,
born Nov. 17th, 1848. These all survived their parents.

My wife was named for her grandmother Dinwiddie

and her grandmother Woods. Her grandmother Woods' maiden name was Charity Dyzart.

After we went to house-keeping, my wife's sister Mary spent most of her time with us, until her mother's death, and went to school in Huntingdon. She was a handsome, fine-looking girl. I have no recollection of ever seeing her out of temper.

James studied law with me. Soon after his father's death he married Miss Susan Porter, a cousin. She was a very lovely girl. How I regretted to hear of her death!

Levi S. Woods was the son of John Woods, and he the son of Samuel Woods. Samuel Woods' father came from Ireland to North Carolina. Judge Gideon B. Black, now of Trenton, Tenn., a grandson of Samuel Woods, to whom I am indebted for the facts relating to Samuel Woods and his children, is not certain whether Samuel was born before or after his father left Ireland. I have not been able to learn the name of Samuel Woods' father, or the date of his imigration to this country. Samuel Woods moved from North Carolina to Kentucky. The date of this removal I have not been able to fix with satisfaction to myself. Judge Black thinks it was in 1773; but from historical facts in relation to the settlement of Kentucky, I think this date must be too early by several years. I will make some further allusion to the time of his removal, when I have concluded what I have to say of his children. He settled in what is now

Madison County, Kentucky. Samuel Woods had the following children, in the order named : (1.) Oliver, the oldest, born about 1764 or 1765. He was killed by the Indians. (2.) Martha, who married John Dyzart. They had four children, two sons and two daughters, the oldest boy named John. (3.) Jane, who married John Herron. They had four children, one girl, who married her cousin John Dyzart, and John, William and Frank Herron. With the sons I was well acquainted. (4.) Margaret, who married Thomas Black. This marriage took place in Kentucky, August 20th, 1793. Of this marriage there were twelve children, among them Newton Black and Judge Gideon B. Black, who was the youngest, born Feb. 4th, 1816. (5.) John Woods was their next child. He was born April 21st, 1771, and died August 26th, 1846. These dates as to John Woods are taken from family records. (6.) The next was Samuel, who married Ann Perviance. (7.) His next child was David, who married a Miss McLary. They had several sons, who moved to Arkansas. (8.) His next, Daniel T. who married a Miss Reese. They had several children, among them Leroy, a distinguished Cumberland Presbyterian preacher. (9.) His next son was called Oliver, after his brother who was killed by the Indians. (10.) His last child, a daughter named Folly, married John Holmes. They had several children, among them John, William and Samuel Holmes.

Samuel Woods' first wife was a Holmes. He married in North Carolina. Judge Black thinks this marriage took place about 1760; I should think a few years later. After the death of his first wife, he married a second time, but had no children by his last wife.

When Samuel Woods went to Kentucky, Judge Black says he carried all his family with him, except his then youngest child, Margaret, Black's mother, who was about two years old; that he returned for her, and during his absence his son Oliver was killed by the Indians, as stated. Some neighbor boys and his son Oliver were together; they heard what they took to be dogs barking, as if they had brought something to bay. They went in the direction of the barking. Indians in ambush fired upon them and killed Oliver; the others escaped. I suppose the Indians were imitating the barking of dogs to decoy the boys from the house.

My reason for thinking Judge Black must be mistaken as to the date when his grandfather moved to Kentucky is, that it does not agree with historic fact, as to the earlier settlement of Kentucky. In the American edition of the Encyclopædia Britanica it is stated that the first permanent settlement in Kentucky was made at Harrodsburgh, in 1774. (See Article " Kentucky "; also Edward S. Ellis' Life of Boone, page 53.) The fort at Boonsboro was completed in the autumn of 1774. (Same author, page

60) On page 64, Boone is made to say that his wife
and daughter were the first white women who ever
"stood upon the banks of the wild and beautiful Kentucky River." Boone reached Boonsboro with his
family in the fall of 1774. These authorities are in
harmony with my former reading upon this subject,
and lead me to conclude that Judge Black must be
mistaken as to the date when his grandfather, Samuel
Woods, moved with his family to Kentucky. I incline
to think the removal must have taken place at some
time between the fall of 1775 and the year 1778. I
simply throw out these suggestions. Unless some
written evidence can be had, the precise date of the
removal will always be in doubt. Judge Black is
remarkable for his recollection of family names, facts
and dates. If he is in error as to the dates to which
I have referred, I should hardly think the error began
with him, but with his ancestors, from whom he
received his information.

Samuel Woods lived in Kentucky until about 1800,
when he moved to Williamson County, Tennessee,
and settled on Harpeth Lick. He afterwards moved
to the home of his son Samuel, who lived near Mc-
Lemoresville, Carroll County, Tennessee, where he
died about 1825. He was, as I understood, largely
over eighty years of age when he died. He was of
Scotch-Irish descent, and a Presbyterian. Judge
Black tells me he was a member of the Paint Lick
church in Kentucky, and that one David Rice
preached at this church.

My Wife's Paternal Ancestry.—John Woods, son of Samuel Woods, my wife's grandfather, was married three times. His first wife was Charity Dyzart. They were married Nov. 9th, 1799. She was born June 22d, 1778, and died Nov. 14th, 1814. His second wife, Margaret Dyzart, sister of his first wife was born Nov. 18th, 1780; died Sept. 25th, 1825. They were married Nov. 14th, 1815. His third wife was Mrs. Hester Ann Craven, born Oct. 15th, 1788. There were no children by this third marriage.

His children were: Levi S., born Sept. 1st, 1801, died Nov. 1st, 1857. Harvey, his second son, born February, 1804, died August, 1864, in Mississippi; he was a Presbyterian preacher. Dyzart, his third son, born Jan. 21st, 1806, died Feb. 8th, 1882, in Arkansas. Margaret, his oldest daughter, was born in February, 1808, and died Nov. 14th, 1865; she married Dr. Drake; she died at her home near Lavenia, Carroll County, Tennessee. Nancy, his second daughter, was born June, 9th, 1810, and died Aug. 14th, 1848; she married her cousin, John Herron—Herron lived near Spring Creek, Madison County, Tennessee, at the time of his death. A daughter, Syrena, born May 3d, 1812, died July 16th, 1824. John Woods, Jr. born Nov, 9th, 1814, died April 19th, 1841, in the neighborhood of Hickory Flat, Carroll County, Tennessee; he left a daughter, an only child, who was called Mat, and who was at our house several times after we were married; she married Dr. Taliaferro,

living in Paris, Tenn.; they went to Texas. These
were the children of John Woods, Sr., by his first
wife.

The children of his second wife were: Carey H.
Woods, born Aug. 29th, 1816, died July 17th, 1885,
in Middle Tennessee; Charity, who married Dr. Clark,
born April 12th, 1818, died Sept. 1st, 1843, in the
neighborhood of Hickory Flat; David H. Woods,
born Oct. 28th, 1822, died Dec. 13th, 1874, in Tipton
County, Tennessee; William H. Woods, born July
25th, 1825, died January, 1850, in California. For
the dates of births and deaths of John Woods and his
children I am indebted to Mrs. Mary Woods, now of
Texas, a daughter of Carey Woods and wife of Andrew
Woods, a brother of my wife. When she visited
Middle Tennessee in the summer of 1891, she copied
them from the family record of John Woods and sent
them to me. As stated in the preface to this little
family sketch, I have left it to my children and the
younger members of my wife's family to collect and
preserve the more recent facts of our families. To
have attempted more on my part would have imposed
to great a tax upon me in my broken-down condition.

John Woods moved to Carroll County in 1819.
He was one of the first settlers. He first settled on
what afterwards became the stage road leading from
Huntingdon to Jackson, and about 12 miles from
Huntingdon. When I first knew the place, it was
generally known as the "old Woods stand." He

afterwards moved to the place near Hickory Flat, where he lived until his death. His son, Carey H., lived on it after him, until he sold to James H. Laneir a few years after the war.

I learned from Col. Woods that when his father moved to West Tennessee there were no grist-mills in the county, and that they had to send to Trace Creek, across Tennessee River, for meal or to have their corn ground. The country was then full of game. Deer, bears and wild turkeys were abundant. There was no trouble about getting meat; the difficulty was to get bread. Col. Woods was about eighteen years old when his father came to Carroll County: "Matthew Henry's Commentaries," that I now have, belonged to John Woods, and after his death to his son, Levi S. The spectacles I gave Silas, to have refilled and mended, also belonged to him. I accidentally broke the glasses out of them a few years ago. I never knew John Woods, though my father had been in the county more than ten years before his death. Being an old Presbyterian. I am told he did not believe in shouting; but it was no uncommon thing for him to come home from church in a shouting frame of mind. I learned from Cass that he was a very pious, godly, upright man.

Samuel Woods and James Dinwiddie, my wife's great-grandfather, became acquainted while they lived in Kentucky. The older members of their families were also acquainted,, and in this way Col.

Woods was led to visit his future father-in-law's house after they came to Tennessee, and became acquainted with his daughter and married her.

After I was married I became acquainted with Mrs. Drake. She was a very sprightly, companionable lady, full of life. She was a very superior woman, full of energy, and possessed rare business qualities. I was very favorably impressed with her.

She died soon after the close of the war. My wife went to see her after the war. I did not see her for several years before her death.

I first visited my future father-in-law's house during Christmas week, 1849, in company with John Boyd. Col. Woods was living on John's Branch, First District of Carroll County. He had an excellent home. Cass was not at home; she was on a visit to her relatives in Henry County. We stayed all night and left the next morning. I liked the appearance of things. As I was about leaving, I handed Col. Woods a book, and told him he might put it in his book-case and give it to his daughter when she returned. My daughter Nannie now has the little book. I at the time was attending to a law-suit for Col. Woods. I had met his daughter Cass at Huntingdon, and was slightly acquainted with her.

Boyd and Col. Woods were Democrats, I a Whig. Boyd was the Sheriff of Carroll County, and as he told me was in the habit of calling at Woods' when in that part of the county. As we were riding off, I said : "John, I like the way things look at this place; you must come with me here again before a great while." Some time about the first of March we went a second time. Cass was at home. John left next morning on business—believe I stayed till evening. Before leaving I said to Miss Woods: "I will be passing to Jackson early in April, and with your permission I will call." She consented, and I did so. After this I made it convenient to have business in that part of the country quite often. I had visited her but a few times before I proposed to her to become a member of the firm. I told her, while talking on the subject, that I was much of my time from home; that she would have to run the house, while I ran the law branch of the concern. We agreed to unite our fortunes for life. But a word passed between Col. Woods and myself upon the subject of my and his daughter's marriage. He gave his consent. I told him I would like to see Mrs. Woods before leaving. She came into the parlor. I took my seat to the left and a little in front of her. I recollect well how I was sitting. I asked her consent to our marriage. She was entirely self possessed, but her countenance indicated seriousness when she entered the room. Her conversation with me upon the subject was a very proper one for the occasion; a shade of seriousness coloring her remarks. Towards its close she spoke of the risk girls took in marrying; saying that their happiness de-

pended entirely upon the conduct of the husband.
She repeated and emphasized this idea. Mrs. Woods
had, I think, done all the talking up to this time. I
had been silent. I then said to her: " Mrs. Woods,
you don't think the risk is all on the part of your
daughter, do you? Don't you suppose there is some
on my part also? I propose making your daughter a
good husband. I think I know something of the
duties the relation will impose on me. If your
daughter's happiness will in a great measure be in
my hands, will not mine be equally so in her hands?"

My remarks dispelled all her seriousness; her face
brightened up; she smiled and became quite cheerful. Indeed, I am not sure she did not laugh. I
have frequently thought of this little incident between my mother-in-law and myself and have always
been inclined to smile at the manner in which the
subject passed off.

We were married, as I have already stated, on the
2d of October, 1850. In about two or three weeks
after we were married, I said to Cass, " Would you
not like to go and see your parents?" She had not
suggested it to me, but I knew she would like to see
home. So we went to see the family. I said to Mrs.
Woods while there, " I knew Cass would like to see
you all, though she had not said so much to me. She
felt, I suppose, that such a suggestion might be a little hasty on her part." We spent a couple of dasy
with the family. On leaving I said to Mrs. Woods,

" I cannot always command my time ; my business
takes me from home a great deal, as you know. Cannot say when I will be here again; but Cass shall
come and see you as often as she may wish." It was
some months after this before Cass and I went together to see her parents. Cass had, however, in
the meantime visited home. While on this visit I
made it convenient to say something like this to Mrs.
Woods, in a rather low tone, as though I did not
wish Cass to hear me; in her presence, however,
knowing that she would hear me : " This girl you gave
me is getting the upper hand of me pretty fast. I
think she is taking a right good start in this direction." I can't call up the exact language I used; but
I tried as delicately as I could to carry with it the
idea that I would be much obliged if she would
speak a kind word for me. Mrs Woods smiled; she
no doubt thought of the conversation we had in the
parlor when I asked her for her daughter. Some
people may talk of " mothers-in-law ;" but I always
loved my mother-in-law; I love to think of her; I
love her memory. Mrs. Woods was a lady of fine
sense. She was full of energy, and an excellent
housewife. She had a great deal of family pride.
You could not be at her home without seeing
that she excelled as a business woman. Everything
about her home bore the evidence of her industry
She favored her father very much. I have rarely
seen a more striking resemblance between father

and daughter. I formed the opinion that she also
bore a strong resemblance to her father in point of
character. She was quick tempered, but always
cheerful and pleasant. She had nothing stubborn or
sullen in her composition.

Col. Woods in his earlier days was fond of keeping
hounds about him, and would occasionally engage in
the chase. He had a couple of young hounds, after
moving to John's Branch, that he thought a good
deal of. They were in the habit of sucking eggs and
breaking up Mrs. Woods' hens' nests. They one day
broke up a hen's nest. Mrs. Woods in a passion, as
well she might be, said to a man whom Col. Woods
had employed about some work at the house: " If
you will take those young dogs out and hang them, I
will give you two bits." He did so. Col. Woods
made rather a long face about his dogs, but said
nothing to Mrs. Woods about them. When he settled with the man for his work he left out the two
bits for hanging the dogs. The man said to him:
" You have forgotten the two bits Mrs. Woods prom-
sed me for killing the dogs." He paid them without
a word. I have heard Cass tell this several times.
It is doubtful whether her mother was in earnest
about having the dogs killed. She made the remark
in a passion, not thinking perhaps that the man
would take her at her word.

Col. Woods was a man of fine personal appearance. He was about six feet high, and slightly cor-

pulent when I first knew him. His features were
highly intellectual. He would have been readily
picked out in any company as no ordinary man. He
was one of the most sensible men I ever knew. He
was well balanced; his character was finely rounded
off. He seemed to have entire control of all his
conduct. He understood human nature, and exercised a large share of influence in the community in
which he lived. I never heard him say or do anything that was not characterized by propriety and
good sense. I was never with him a day without
feeling I had been benefitted in some way or other.
He was a very affectionate husband. I have heard
my wife say she never at any time heard her father
give her mother a cross or unkind word.

He and Mr. W. W. Herron were for some years
engaged in the mercantile business as partners, at
Hickory Flat. They then went to Henry County,
Tennessee, some miles north of Paris, where they
continued their enterprise. After this they moved
to Huntingdon, where they continued as partners
for a few years. When they discontinued business
in Henry County, Col. Woods moved to his farm on
John's Branch, Carroll Co., where he had a large
body of land. I have heard Col. Woods and my wife
speak of the year he moved to John's Branch. I
think it was in 1810 or 1812. His house was situated
on a little bluff, that ran up to the branch. At the
foot of this bluff was a fine spring, not more than a

stone's cast from the north end of the house. I was always charmed with the location.

We boarded for several months after marrying, with C. S. Wood, of Huntingdon, before we went to housekeeping. (He was not related to my father-in-law.)

✗ David Bell married Mary Dinwiddie, daughter of my wife's grandfather, by his second wife. We kept house together the first year after marriage.

I and my wife had the following children : Silas B. born July 26th, 1851; Nannie J., born April 3d, 1854 LeGrand W., born May 31st, 1856; Lizzie H., born February 18th, 1859; Paul, born January 31st, 1861; Clopton, born March 7th, 1864; Georgie Mai, born October 18th, 1868, and Doddridge, born September 18th, 1870.

The last of June and first of July, 1851, I had to attend my river courts, and I hesitated very much about leaving home. I talked to Dr. Wright; told him that I hated to leave home; that I expected my wife would be confined within a month. He told me to go on to my courts and be cheerful about it. He had no idea my wife would need me before I got back. I talked to Cass; told her that I did not like to leave home at such a time. She told me to attend my courts; she felt no uneasiness at my leaving. I told her that Dr. Wright promised me that every attention should be paid her, if needed during my absence, and that a messenger would be sent for me should it be necessary. I went to my courts, but was uneasy and unhappy all the time. I got back two weeks or more before her confinement. It was a great relief to me to find I was at home on time. Neither my wife nor I had any relations living in Huntingdon, save David Bell and his wife. Mary was a little younger than my wife. Being so much of my time from home, it would have been a great relief to me had either of us any older relatives living in the place. I often felt the want of this.

In the spring of 1853 our nurse took the measles. We could never account for the manner in which she took them, unless from some person passing on the street. I was compelled to attend Supreme Court at Jackson. The nurse was recovering when I started. I saw Dr. Wright, and he promised to watch my family. He thought that neither Silas nor his mother could take them and get very bad off before I could get back. I went by my mother's, and she promised to go up and stay a few days, or until my return. I got through my business at Jackson and late Saturday night I reached Col. Woods', on my way home. Sunday morning after breakfast my horse was brought around. The Colonel insisted that I should spend the day, or stay until evening with them. My answer was: "If I would spend the day with you, under the circumstances, you ought to lose all respect for me, and I would certainly lose my own self-respect." I reached home about noon.

The nurse had gotten about well. Silas had taken
the measles after I left, and was about well; and his
mother had taken them a day or two before my return. Dr. Wright came up in the evening. He said
my wife was doing well enough, but thought it best
from her symptoms to bleed her. Cass never had
much fancy for having any one cutting about her,
and so she would not consent to be bled. The next
morning Dr. Wright still insisted that she needed
blood-letting. He said that while there was nothing
serious in her case, he was satisfied that the best
course was to bleed her. I told the doctor to get
out his lancet. I dropped off my coat and shoes and
slipped into bed behind her, and said to her, " Now,
Cass, lay yourself upon my bosom and shut your
eyes; this is about the best place you will ever find
to die." The doctor bled her, and she was up and
about in a few days.

In the fall of 1863 I left my home in Huntingdon
and moved to my plantation lying on the railroad,
three or four miles north of Trezevant. I stayed in
Huntingdon about as long as I well could. It was
difficult to keep family supplies. I frequently had
Federal soldiers to feed. Some of these I found to
be honest, good men, and some the reverse. I was
never troubled with soldiers on my plantation.

My land, Brother Silas' and Brother Moses' ad-
joined. Our houses were but a short distance apart.
But for the troubles of the war, the two years I lived

on my farm would have been among the most pleasant of my life. When the war ended I was very much embarrassed as to what I should do. I felt very much broken up as to my future plans. I hesitated as to what step I should take. Should I remain upon my plantation, or buy a small place near Trezevant, and there educate my children, and in this way start them off in life? or should I go to the law? Finally, as the way opened up, I determined to return to the practice of my profession. I thought of locating in Jackson, Memphis or Trenton. There were some reasons why I preferred Jackson. It was more convenient to my river courts; but there were objections that overbalanced this. I thought I could perhaps make more money in Memphis for a time, but then the thought of bringing up my family in a city, especially if my boys should not be grown and settled in their habits and in business when I should be taken from them, was repulsive to me. I never had much fancy for city life any way. After weighing the subject as well as I could, I decided in favor of Trenton. I first bought a place in town from Esq. William Kelton. I preferred, however, a country home, reasonably convenient to my office, when I bought of Kelton. After buying of Kelton, James A. McDearmon proposed selling, and I bought his place lying on the Eaton Road, one and one-half miles west of Trenton. I did not want to bring up my boys in town. I had seen so many town boys run the road

to ruin, that I feared the result. I would necessarily
be much of my time from home, and the children
would in a great measure be left entirely under control of their mother. I always had a fondness for
plantation life, and in my earlier married days I
looked forward with pleasure to the time when I
could pretty well give up the law, and settle down
with my wife and children in some pleasant country
home.

In the last days of December, 1865, I moved to the
place mentioned, bought of McDearmon. The older
children will remember something of the time we
had on the road, the first day. It commenced rain-
ing soon after we started in the morning, and rained
heavily until nearly night. It was a gloomy day, and
my feelings were very much in harmony with the day·
The bridges on the leading roads were down, and we
had to take a circuitous route, leaving old Shady
Grove and Milan to the right. Rutherford's Fork
had become almost impassable from the heavy rains,
before we reached it. The bottom for several hundred yards was covered with water. I hesitated
about attempting to cross. My family was in a small
two-horse wagon, drawn by two old mules. I ordered the boy who was driving to hold up. The water
looked so threatening that I should have turned
back; but there was no house within a mile or two
at which we could spend the night, and the roads
had also become almost impassable. I was on horse

back. I knew but little of the road through the bottom, but concluded that I would ride through the water and see if the wagon with my family could go safely over. I endeavored to go through and keep in the road from the marks on the trees. I had gone about half the distance to the bridge, I suppose, when I met a young Mr. Robertson crossing from the opposite side, driving a team of four large, fine mules. The wagon and team belonged to J. M. Coulter. Robertson knew me. I had known his father for many years. I asked him what the chances were for my getting safely across. He said if I knew the route well I could make it; but if not, it would be attended with some hazard— that I might get my family swamped in some of the sloughs. He was acquainted with the way, and proposed to drive over and take my family across, and let my wagon follow his. When he got across he took out his two lead mules, and left them with a young man who was with him. I put my family in his wagon, and we all got safely through the water. I think he made no charge; but I paid him two dollars, or two dollars and fifty cents—do not recollect which. I never paid any money more cheerfully in my life. I stayed that night with Major Bryant, of whom I have already spoken. He entertained us most hospitably. I have always felt that there was something providential in my meeting young Robertson just at the time and place I did. It was at a time

and place I least expected meeting any one. Had I
not met him I might have attempted passing through
the water with my family, and might have met with
some accident. Should my sons Silas and LeGrand
read these lines, they will understand something
they did not and could not well have understood
twenty years ago.

When I reached the end of my journey, the second
night, after dark, with my wife and children all safe,
I felt decidedly relieved. Having to change my
home in the broken-up and unsettled state of the
country, made this a rather dark period for me; but
after settling down in our new home, hope came
back to me, and I said to my wife: "Cass, my heart
has returned to me. Do your best management with
our domestic matters, and I will put in all my
strength at the law." My wife always knew how to
clothe her family with but little expense; and for
several years we both determined to visit the stores
as seldom as possible. I recollect my wife wore a
mixed dress, after we came to Trenton, that she had
made at Valley Farm. She always looked handsome
to me in that dress. I also wore my jeans for a year
or two after we came to Trenton.

I heard many persons say, before and after the
commencement of the war, that they wanted it put
off in their day; they did not want it to come on in
their day. I always felt and said, if it had to come
and was an event in the near future, let it come on

in my day, let it fall upon me, and not upon my children. This is the way I felt, and this is what I always said, from the beginning to the end of the war; and I am now glad that its sorrows and troubles fell upon me, rather than upon my children.

During the last years of the war, dry goods became very scarce, especially cotton goods. They were exceedingly high. I think I paid as much as eighty cents to a dollar a yard for calico, the last year of the war.

After we went to Valley Farm, my wife brought the spinning-wheel and loom into use. She was spinning one day, and I said to her: "Wife, how handsome and graceful you look at the spinning-wheel!" She said there was not so much grace and beauty about it: that it was the idea of her being at work that was so pleasing to me. A day or two after this I was reading Kame's Elements of Criticism, and came across what he said about there being something pleasing to the eye and mind in motion and force applied to the industrial pursuits of life; that "the Creator in his goodness to us had so ordered it; otherwise labor would be repulsive, and we would turn from it in disgust." I read to her what he said on this subject, and remarked: "If you will not agree with me, Lord Kame does."

I never knew a more conscientious person than my wife. There was no deception, no guile in her composition. Some time before we were married, I

was talking with her on the subject, when she said
to me: " I am at times troubled with a sudden weakness that passes over me. Did you not see me sit
down on the floor a few minutes while straightening
up the parlor this morning? A weak feeling passed
over me, and I had to sit down. I could not marry
a man without telling him of it." Her manner of
telling me, and the fact that a girl could do so under
the circumstances, made a singular impression on
my mind. This nervous weakness troubled her for
a year or two after we were married, and then for
many years she was hardly ever troubled with it.

My wife professed religion when she was quite a
girl; and for a time, as she told me, her hope was
bright and she enjoyed religion. She did not join
the church for some time after making a profession.
For much of her time she lived a doubting Christian.
She thought if she had joined the church earlier she
would never have been troubled with so many
doubts. As to her own merits, she was always
clothed with the garments of humility. For several
years before her death we seldom, if ever, passed a
day together without conversing upon the subject of
religion. I always tried to encourage and comfort
her, and hold her head above the waves. I would
point her to the promises of the Bible. She was
well read in the Scriptures, and was greatly inclined
not to take the promises to herself. "They are for
others, not for me," she would say. I recollect one

day she was talking to me in a desponding way, and I said to her, "Cass, would you take the reins out of the hands of your Heavenly Father?" Her quick reply was, "No! no!" I used to tell her that, had she been in the place of the Christian pilgrim mentioned in the song, when Apollyon told him his captain had gone before and he would see his face no more, she would, I supposed, have agreed with him, and would have given up the journey. She was very fond of Pilgrim's Progress, and said she was very much like Bunyan. Mr. Little Faith was an interesting character to her. His faith, though little and feeble, was still faith, she would say. My wife at all times felt great solicitude for the salvation of our children. For years before her death, this desire would at times be intense. Her heart was burdened for their salvation. She would ask me to pray for them—"Pray for them with all your heart! pray for them like Brother Silas used to pray for you!" I would try to comfort her about our children, and refer to the fact that Silas and some of the others had professed. I often said to her at such times, "Mamma, I have a goodly hope that the Lord in his mercy will in some way bring all our children into his fold. Try to be hopeful; don't be desponding."

In the winter before her death, she became concerned about Lizzie. It was painful to see the intensity of her feelings. She pleaded with me to pray for her. More than once she said to me: "Mr.

Jones, *I don't feel like I can wait—no time to wait for protracted or revival meetings!*" In a short time Brother Montgomery came along. He was at our house. He had several earnest conversations with Lizzie. Soon after he left, Lizzie made an open profession of religion. In speaking of the fact of her deep concern about Lizzie, I said to her: "Mamma, how can you have such doubts about your own acceptance, when in answer to your prayers the Lord has converted our daughter, and that at a time when we so little expected it? You felt you could not wait. She was the burden of your heart; and here in the winter there comes along a stranger, and our daughter is converted. Pluck up heart, and never again give way to despondency. Never again become a prisoner in Doubting Castle." I felt that Lizzie was converted in answer to the prayers of her mother. Our children are now all converted, except Doddridge, and I have a goodly hope that the Lord in his mercy will sanctify some means to his salvation.*

I do not know that a day has passed over my head since I had children that I did not pray for them. I believe in prayer. The first night we spent at our boarding-house, after we were married, I said to Cass: "It has been my intention when I married to hold family prayers." It pleased her. We read a chapter and knelt together in prayer.

* Since the above was written, Doddridge has professed religion and has been baptized. The Lord be praised!

My wife, without possessing the strongest constitution, was rarely in bed from illness. I was twelve or
thirteen years her senior, and in the course of nature
I thought of nothing but her surviving me. But she
always said otherwise. She never expected to live
to be old.

Up to within eight or ten months of her death, her
health had for several years been very good. I felt
she would probably live to be old. She had a chill
in September, 1877. None of the older children
were about the house. I was scarcely able to wait
on her. Her nervous system seemed to give way
under the effects of the chill. Several times she
asked me if she was not dying. I told her she was
not, and bore up as cheerfully as I could in my feeble
condition. I sent for Dr. Levy immediately when
her chill came on; but before he arrived the effects
had pretty well passed off. After this I felt a good
deal of solicitude about her health, and watched her
with no little anxiety. I talked with Dr. Levy pri-
vately, and told him the way the chill affected her
made me feel serious. The next day she was up and
about; and while there was no apparent reason why
I should feel any particular anxiety about her condition, yet I could not help feeling so. I requested Dr.
Levy to keep her on the best course of tonics;
which he did. I thought she needed tonic treatment. I could see, for a year or two before her
death, that time had made some little impression

upon her. She did not appear quite as young as in former years. Not long after Lizzie professed religion, my wife in conversation said to me one day : " I feel like my life work is accomplished." I passed off the remark in some light manner, but it saddened me. I could not help feeling sad at the remark.

For three consecutive Sundays before my wife's death, she attended church and seemed to enjoy the sermons more than usual, and appeared quite cheerful. Brother Hillsman was our pastor. On one of these occasions—I think it was the last Sunday—the subject was, " We all have our burdens to bear." She spoke of the sermon, and seemed more than usually cheerful in speaking of it. In the evening, after returning from church, she had a slight chill, or chilly sensation. She took, the next morning, what quinine we thought necessary to guard against its return. While her health had remained reasonably good during the winter and spring, she occasionally, and but occasionally, was troubled with coldish depressing spells. It was not thought best to give much quinine at such times, but in connection with small portions of quinine to give stimulants and tonics.

Monday morning she got up as usual, dressed and cooked a young chicken, and sent it to Nannie by the children as they went to school. Nannie was a little unwell. In the evening my wife had another chill, but nothing serious about it. I did not, however, like its return. That night and the next morning I increased the quantity of quinine. Tuesday evening she had another slight chill. Wednesday morning I remarked to her, "I believe I will send for the doctor." She answered, "No, you will not send for the doctor for me; I need no doctor." I had given her during the morning four quinine pills, containing from two to two and one-half grains of quinine each. She seemed doing very well, and was entirely cheerful. A little before twelve o'clock I wanted her to take another pill. She felt so well that she smiled and said, "I don't think I need it, but I will take it, for should I not do so, and have a chill, you will think if I had taken it I would not have had the chill." I really did not think she needed the last pill, but wanted her to be on the safe side. I suggested to her to remain in bed Tuesday and Wednesday, which she did. She kept her Testament (the one Mr. Landis had given her) in bed with her, and would read from time to time.

In a short time after taking the last pill, the chill came on her again, more severe in form. I at once felt alarmed, though I kept my fears to myself. I sent for Dr. Happel. He was not long in getting out. Her symptoms during the evening increased my fears. Towards night the doctor proposed going home, and spoke of returning in the morning if I thought it necessary. I told him if he went home he must return that night, which he did. Her stomach

seemed a good deal irritated. She frequently made
efforts to vomit. Thursday morning Dr. Happe
went back to town, and returned in an hour or two]
and when he went back about the middle of the day,
I told him, while I had every confidence in his treatment, to bring Dr. Levy with him in the evening.
Dr. Levy came out with him. I told Cass, as the
doctors were coming to the house, that I had direct-
ed Happel to bring Levy with him. She spoke of it
as being entirely unnecessary. I remarked that I
supposed she was correct, but it was a little matter,
and I thought I might be indulged in it. When the
doctors came in the room, I spoke of what I had said
to my wife, and her reply; that I had said to her I
proposed to pay the bills, and thought I might be
permitted to have my own way, if it was any pleasure
to me. She seemed cheerful, and I think smiled at
my remark. The irritation about the stomach increased, if anything, attended with a good deal of
thirst and a burning sensation. I procured ice for
her; perhaps it was Friday before I got the ice.
She had no chill after Wednesday. Thursday I told
the doctors I felt very serious about my wife, and
that one or the other must remain with her continually. They did so. I felt that she would not recover.
My heart sank within me. I suggested to the doctors that evening that I would send for Silas, but
they said it was entirely unnecessary. They may
have so answered to quiet my fears. Friday morn-

ing I had Silas dispatched for. He reached home
on Saturday a little after noon. His mother recognized him and put her arms around his neck. In a
few hours after his arrival she became pretty much
unconscious; indeed, the quinine she had taken
made her almost entirely deaf. I was saying something to her, and she told me she was so deaf she
could not understand me. In my shattered nervous
condition, I could not stay in the room and wait on
her all the time as I wished. It was physically im-
possible. How painful it was not to be able to
remain at her side and be with her to the last! She
died Sunday morning, May 13th, 1878, about three
o'clock. Drs. Happel and Levy did everything that
could be done, as I thought. The first three chills
(or chilly sensations, for they could hardly be called
chills,) were very slight. There was nothing in them,
considered in themselves, to excite alarm. After
the recurrence of the chill on Wednesday, I thought
had I given larger quantities of quinine from the
first, combined with iron and nux vomica, it might
have stimulated and toned up her system and saved
her life. I have often thought this; but perhaps we
never lose a member of our family, except in case of
extreme old age, without thinking that, had a different course of treatment been pursued, or something
additional done, a different result would or might
have followed.

The longer I have lived, the better have I been

satisfied that I married the right woman. Had I life
to go over again, I would go to the same home and
marry the same girl. We are told by inspired wisdom that a prudent wife is from the Lord; and if a
prudent wife is from the Lord, surely a good mother
is from the Lord.

When my wife was no more, a feeling of inexpress-
ible loneliness possessed me. There seemed to be a
void within and about me. We may be in the busy,
bustling world; we may even be surrounded by
friends, and yet we may be truly alone. We may at
such times feel that the hand of desolation is upon
us. It was hard for me to realize that my wife was
no more. For months after her death, whenever I
rode out from home and would be returning, I had a
strange feeling that she would meet me on reaching
the house. This was, I suppose, from long associa-
tion. I would be willing, under the blessing of
Heaven, to go over my married life again. With my
present experience I think I could in some respects
better it; but it would in the main have to be about
what it was. I would not be willing to undertake to
raise my children again. Not that I would so much
shrink from the labor and care of raising a family;
but the responsibility is so great, the task so deli-
cate, that I should fear that my errors in this respect
might be greater and more numerous than they were.

The law of love should be the rule of the household.
We should learn to forbear with each other, and to

bear one another's burdens. We should always re member that others have their burdens as well as we. It is in the commonplace duties of life, with its ever-recurring petty trials, that we need to be watch ful. It is to meet these cheerfully and courageously that we especially need the grace of God.

Few mothers possess the happy talent of govern ing and training children so well as did my wife. With her it seemed to be a natural gift, rather than an acquired art. If our children prove to be worthy men and women to the end, it will, I am sure, be mainly due to their early maternal training. I was much of the time from home, and the governing and training of our children devolved largely upon their mother.

My wife was a very strict observer of the Sabbath. I always thought I was strict enough; but she kept a little in advance of me in this respect. I thought she stood so straight that she leant back a little. I I more than once reminded her of the boy who, as a means of encouraging him to be good, respect the Sabbath and reach the better land, was told it was always Sunday there, and who answered, "I don't want to go where it is always Sunday!" I reckon the little fellow thought he had had enough of Sun day in this world.

In speaking of my wife, it will be seen that I have occasionally used the word "Mamma." In my later days, when none but the family were present, I frequently chimed in with the children and called her "Mamma." She called me to account for this one day; but I insisted that it was an affectionate way of addressing her in the home circle. I said, " I never indulge in this way of addressing you, except when none are present but the children." After this she never complained at my thus addressing her. She also in our later years frequently called me " Papa."

My wife was a little over medium size; not so tall as her sister Mary, or sister Georgie. Nannie's face resembles her mother's more than any of her daughters. Her profile, a little turned from you, has a striking likeness to her mother's. Of the boys, I think Silas' features most like his mother's. I have already stated that my wife was eminently conscientious. She was so by nature. She was brought up by Christian parents, around whose hearth the domestic virtues were cultivated and had their abode. She knew nothing of dissimulation, and was a stranger to artifice and affectation. Good sense was the predominant feature of her character, and its controlling element. She was eminently discreet and well balanced. The conscientious discharge of all the duties of domestic life was with her an absorbing consideration.

SILAS P. JONES.—Brother Silas married Miss Jane Gallion on Oct. 13th, 1841. He died August 21st, 1876. He was set apart by the Baptist church

at McLemoresville to the work of the Gospel ministry when he was a little over thirty years of age.
Elder J. M. Hurt and Dr. J. R. Graves constituted
the presbytery that ordained him to this work. He
was a man of fine personal appearance, being a little
over six feet high and well proportioned. He and
Brother Isaac resembled each other very much. He
was not a metaphysician; he never dealt in abstrac-
tions or subtleties of doctrine. He was a man of
thorough good sense, plain and practical. He possessed a warm heart, active sympathies, a generous
and noble nature. He was frank and cordial, highly
companionable, and was always hopeful and cheerful.
There was a good deal of magnetism in his composition. I always felt strengthened by being with him.
He entered readily into the feelings and sympathies
of those around him, and knew how to say a kind
and sympathizing word to the afflicted or distressed.
He possessed strong convictions, and was true to
his convictions. His education was confined to the
ordinary English branches, such as were taught in
the schools of the country in his days. He was
raised on the plantation; his life had been given exclusively to the business of the farm. He had never
been in public life when he began preaching, and was
entirely unaccustomed to public speaking. I was
not a little affected at his undertaking to preach. I
felt satisfied, however, that he entered upon this
course only from a sense of duty. I believe in a

special call to the ministry; and believing this, I believed that the Lord would sustain him and make him useful. His labors were blessed, and he was in the hands of the Lord the means of turning many to righteousness. If ever I reach the heavenly land, of which I have an humble hope, I feel that, under God, he was the means of leading me in the good and right way. Save my mother, my own wife and children, there was no one on earth that I felt so near and dear to me. He received but little for preaching. Not long after the war, he told me that, with the exception of one or two years, he had given away about as much as had ever been given him for his ministerial labors. I had it in my power to be helpful to him in some respects; and that I had the ability, and the will to use it, has always afforded me the sincerest satisfaction. He told me, after he had been preaching some years, that when he first commenced praying in public it always embarrassed him, until he was called upon one day to pray at a camp-meeting held near Shady Grove. This was before he began preaching. While praying, the presence and love of God became so manifested to him that he began shouting and praising God. "If the assembled universe had been present," he said to me, "I would have praised God my Saviour." He was willing for all to be present, men and angels. After this he never felt any embarrassment in praying in public. I felt that this manifestation of God's presence and

love was granted him for the purpose of strengthen-
ing his faith and removing from him the fear of man.
My answer to him was: "You will perhaps while
on earth never again have such a wonderful manifestation of the divine love and approbation."

These wonderful visitations of the presence and
glory of God are not often met with in the life of the
same individual. We have just so much grace and
divine help given us as to enable us to discharge the
duties that God requires at our hands, and no more,
and none to spare. It was so under the Old Testament dispensation; it is so under the New.

My brother, as stated, died on the 21st day of
August, 1876. He wrote me some time in February
that he was seriously ill. I went to see him, and
remained with him, as I remember, two nights and
a day. I was to see him several times, until my own
health gave way in June. The second time I went
to see him, which was in March, he feared that he
had cancer of the stomach. My fears were also
alarmed, but I was reluctant to believe such was the
case. But in the end no room was left for doubt. I
went to see him in April. He was not yet fully satisfied as to the nature of his malady, but still appre-
hended he had cancer of the stomach. He asked
me what I thought of his condition, did I think he
would recover? I said to him that I could not think
he would not recover; that a severe case of dyspep-
sia would account for his symptoms. He told me he

did not fear death; and he at this time was not, I am
sure, satisfied that he would not be restored to
health again. For about two months before his
death I did not see him. I was confined most of that
time closely to my bed. For many years before his
death, to be useful and to do good seemed to be the
ruling purpose of his life.

My brother left the following children : LeGrand
M., born August 1st, 1850; Mary C., born June 25th,
1847, who married Dr. Wingo; Bettie G., born June
25th, 1857, who married a Mr. Askew ; (they are all
living in the neighborhood of Trezevant); Archer,
born September 25, 1853, and died October 4th, 1873.
His eldest son, James M., was born October 1st,
1843.   He enlisted in the confederate service ; was
in the battle fought opposite Columbus, Ky., and
escaped unhurt. He was mortally wounded in the
battle of Shiloh on Sunday.   Brother Isaac brought
him home. I was to see him several times after he
was brought home and before he died, and stayed
with him much of the time.   When I first saw him I
had some hope he would recover from his wounds.
He was struck by a Minie ball, a little below the
region of the stomach, the ball coming out near the
spinal column, which was not injured. He complained of no pain. He died April 19th 1862.

ELDER J. M. HURT.—I cannot close this little
family sketch without saying a few words about

Elder J. M. Hurt. He and my father's family were acquainted in Virginia. I knew him from the time we came to Tennessee until his death. After my father's death he manifested a good deal of interest in our family. He always treated me with marked kindness and respect. I and my brother Silas appreciated him through life with little less than filial regard. He felt great interest in Silas as a young preacher, and was to him as a father in the ministry. I had many evidences of the warm interest he felt in my welfare. He was of great benefit to me, not only in my earlier years, but indeed through life. Left pretty much alone, with no special friend to counsel or guide me, I appreciated more sensibly the interest he manifested in me and my father's family. Whenever I could, I sought his company, and loved to be with him.

I joined the Baptist church at McLemoresville while Elder Hurt was pastor, and he baptized me. He was a well-informed man; and while there were many men of more learning and higher culture, I have always thought he was one of the most intellectual men I ever knew. He was by nature a great man, of masculine common sense, and an original thinker; and was inclined to exhaust any subject in which he became interested. He was not what would be called a polished man; there was something of the rough-hewn about his character. When a young man he read Blackstone's Commentaries, as

I learned from him after I became a lawyer, and at
one time thought of adopting the Law as a profession. Had he done so, he would have taken the
first rank in his profession. He was a man of clear
conceptions, strong convictions, and unswerving integrity. He must have been somewhat advanced in
life before he became a preacher of the Gospel. My
father had been in Tennessee several years before I
heard of Elder Hurt's preaching. He had, as I understood, been ordained to the ministry several
years before I heard him. When called out by an
important occasion, he generally preached a grand
sermon. Our old-fashioned camp-meetings suited
him. Upon such occasions he came nearer John
Keer than any man I ever heard. I once heard him,
at the old camp-meeting ground near Shady Grove,
preach with powerful effect from the text, "There is
a friend that sticketh closer than a brother." I may
judge partially of many of our old men in the ministry. Men of the present day, turned out from our
schools, may have more learning, greater knowledge
of books, and higher culture; but I am slow to
believe that we have that grand class of men that
belonged to the past generation. It seems to me
that men of the present day are less spiritually
minded, and rely more on the knowledge of books,
than men of the past. I by no means depreciate
learning; but may not the too eager pursuit of the
mere learning to be acquired from books chill the

spiritual man, cause the student to rely too much
upon his learning, and leave undeveloped the natural
powers, powers which must always be developed to
make a truly great man?

ELDER GEORGE HARRIS was a Presiding Elder in
the Methodist Church when I first knew him. I
rode out from Huntingdon with him one morning,
six or eight miles on the Trenton road. He was on
his way home, and I was riding out to my mother's.
This was before I was married, and was the beginning of my acquaintance with him. I found him to
be very companionable and interesting. My older
children will recollect him well.

Elder Harris was not a graduate of any of the
schools; his educational advantages in early life
were rather limited; he was self-educated. He may
be said to have been a student through life; was well
read, and possessed a large share of valuable information. He was very much of an independent and
original thinker. His natural gifts were of a high
order. He was eminently practical, and was a man
of fine executive ability. He was resolute and in-
trepid, clear-headed and broad-minded; possessed a
strong will, and was a man of inflexible integrity
He was fitted by nature to be a leader among men.
In person he was plain, simple and unostentatious.
There was no affectation, no dissimulation about
him; nothing narrow or little entered into his char-

acter. He possessed a large share of those qualities of head and heart that command admiration and
esteem. He was frank and cordial, and had many
warm and devoted friends; and those who differed
from him were compelled to respect him.

His long life was well and usefully spent; and he
has left his impress upon the people among whom
for many years he lived and labored. He was a
zealous and indefatigable preacher in the early history of West Tennessee. His labors in the cause of
the Gospel were greatly blessed; many professed
religion under his ministry, and he was the means of
turning many to righteousness. He exercised more
influence in building up his denomination in West
Tennessee than any other single individual. He was
no ordinary preacher; and when his powers were
called out upon some important occasion, generally
preached a grand sermon. I know of no preacher in
his church in West Tennessee that equalled him in
the pulpit; nor can I say that I know of any in the
other denominations that excelled him. There were
in his later days those of his church that were more
scholarly; but, as I have said of J. M. Hurt, I say of
Elder Harris, the schools do not often turn out just
such men as either of them. Their broad, manly
common sense, their knowledge of the heart and
the means of reaching the heart, is something more
than the schools, or mere scholastic training, can
give. Harris knew the character of the people

among whom he lived and labored, knew their spiritual wants, and knew how to adapt himself to them.
I had not been in Trenton long, before he one day
stepped into my office. When he was about leaving
I requested him never to miss an opportunity of
spending a night with me, when he could do so. He
was a fine conversationalist, and I was very fond of
hearing him talk, especially of the history of his
early days. He knew much of the early history of
Tennessee; knew something personally of the later
years of the great Cumberland Revival, and was well
acquainted with numbers who had passed through it.
These were interesting subjects to me, and he was
always ready to engage in conversation on them.
Out of this great revival the Cumberland Presbyterian Church sprang.

There was a good deal of the pioneer in his composition. He was fond of his rifle, and of hunting deer
and bear. Some of his adventures were highly ex-
citing. His cool daring at times was surprising. I
will give one incident, as it illustrates his character
and may interest my grandchildren. Not long after
he came to Henry County, while he was out on the
farm, he one day heard a hog put up a fearful squealing, not far distant from the field in which he was
working. From the terrible outcry of the hog, he
was satisfied that a bear had caught him. He had
his rifle with him; it was loaded and in good condition. He always kept his rifle in good order for any

emergency. Rifle in hand, he started in the direction
of the noise. The cane and undergrowth in the
woods was thick; to avoid these, and to be as silent
as possible, he took to the bed of a dry branch, that
led in the direction in which he heard the hog. The
squealing of the hog became fainter and fainter. As
he approached near, he crept softly along the bed
of the branch; and coming to where the branch
made a sudden turn, he saw the bear on the hog, not
many feet in front of him; my recollection is, not
more than two or three lengths of his rifle. Harris
was in a stooping posture. He and the bear saw
each other about the same time. The bear threw
himself back upon his haunches. Instantly Harris
had his rifle levelled upon him, took aim and fired.
The bear sprang forward, ran over him, knocked off
his hat, and went on his way. Harris-reloaded, followed the trail of the bear, by the blood, and in a few
hundred yards came upon him, and found him dead,
he having given him a mortal shot. I do not think
Daniel Boone or any other border man ever displayed
cooler nerve than Harris did upon this occasion.

CHARLES JONES, *Colored.*—When the war ended,
many of the colored people got new homes. Family
ties were severed. Charles, the colored man of
whom I have spoken in connection with the wonderful meteoric display, moved to Gibson to be with his
wife. In passing to and from Carroll, I had at different times seen most of the old family servants, save

Charles. I had not seen him for several years after
the war. One day he stepped into my office at Trenton. I was alone. We had a long talk. Charles
was undoubtedly affected, and I was too. He spoke
of his "mistiss," my mother; of the fact that she
had raised him from a child, and of his regret that he
had not seen her in her last illness. He had not
heard of her sickness until after her death. When
he was about leaving he said: "Mass LeGrand, I
must hug you before I leave!"—and so he did.
After this, Charles came frequently to see us, until
his death, which was in February, 1886; and at such
times he generally received some substantial evidence of the esteem in which he was held by the
family. He used to make bread-trays for sale in
ante-bellum days. Not long after he first came to
see me, after I moved to Trenton, I told him he
must make me a tray. He did so. My recollection
is that I paid him double the price put on it. It was
made of tupelo gum. I now have it. I want it preserved in the family as an heirloom. Charles was
one of the best men I ever knew. When he died, I
don't think he left a better man behind him, white or
colored. For many years before the war he held
prayers at night. He generally became interested at
such times, and everybody on the place could hear
him pray. Mother felt especially interested in hearing him. I frequently heard her speak of what a
comfort it was to her to hear him pray. I never saw

a man who walked nearer and lived more in commu-
nion with God.

CHARLES CLARK, *Colored.*—I had for six or seven
years before the war owned a colored man named
Charles Clark. I bought him at his own request.
He called on me at my office one day, with a note
from his master saying he would sell him. I told
him to go and see my wife, and if he and she could
agree it would be all right on my part. My wife
wanted me to buy him, stating as her reason, that
with Charles on hand she would always feel easy in
my absence. He was at the time about fifty years
old. He was one of the most reliable men I ever
knew. I never felt uneasy with anything in his
hands; knew it would come up right.

After the Federal soldiers came into the country,
some of the colored people went off with them; but
few of them, however, from our part of the State.
One day I said to Charles: "If you want to leave
me, I don't want you to slip off; there is no necessity
for this; but pack up and come and tell us farewell—
I have something left yet, and I will give you some
money to help you until you can find employment."
Charles said he had no idea of leaving me; that they
(meaning the Federals) would not get him off, unless they tied him and took him by force. In the fall
of 1863 I moved to my plantation, lying on the
railroad, three or four miles north of Trezevant.

Charles was left in charge of my old home. When the war ended I gave him a home for a year free of charge. Two or three years after the close of the war he came to see me, and wanted to live with me, saying he had rather live with me than anybody else. We were all glad to see him; no doubt of this. He stayed with us a day or two, and made his arrangements to live with me; but before the end of the year one of his wife's daughters died, as I learned from him, and this caused such a change in the family that he could not come. This was the last time I saw Charles. He died a few years after this. I did not know he had been sick until I heard of his death, and the news of his departure saddened me.

I had a colored woman who died during the war. My father in law gave her to my wife soon after we were married. Her hand was in mine when she breathed her last.

I have never heard any one say, since the war, that he would have African slavery restored in the Southern States. I am glad its responsibility no longer rests upon me, or is to rest upon my children. Not that I think slavery a sin. Abraham, called the friend of God, was a slaveholder. The Mosaic law recognized slavery. Slavery existed in the days of Christ and his Apostles. The duties of both masters and servants are taught in the New Testament. Paul restored Onesimus, after he was converted, to his master.

In the Southern States, in ante-bellum days, the colored people were better cared for than any purely laboring population of which I have any knowledge. They performed but moderate labor, and were free from the weightier cares that devolved upon their masters; they were taken care of in sickness, and provided for in old age. But when I say this, I frankly confess there were things connected with slavery with which I was never satisfied.

I would not be misunderstood from what I have just said. I believe in the doctrine of State sovereignty. The Constitution of the United States was made by the States, as separate, distinct political communities, each State acting for itself. This the history of the Constitution abundantly establishes: and by its terms it is binding *between the States ratifying the same.* The Federal Government, under the Constitution, is one of delegated powers; its powers are limited, and it can rightfully exercise no powers save those that are delegated. This is so upon principle, and needs no declaration to that effect. But it is, out of abundant caution, so declared in the tenth article of the Amendments to the Constitution. All the décisions of the Supreme Court of the United States, up to 1860, not only recognize but declare these doctrines. Entertaining these opinions, my allegiance went with my State when she withdrew from the Federal Union.

A. TSIN.—My children may at some future day wish to know how I became interested in the little Chinese girl, A. Tsin.

The Chinese were inclined, some years ago, to boycott any of their race who embraced the Christian religion. This feeling still continues. In the September number of the Foreign Missionary Journal of 1884 or 1885, as well as I recollect, there was published a letter from Brother E. Z. Simmons, one of our missionaries to Canton, China. In this letter he said he had recently had a hot and muddy walk, and being tired, had sat down to rest in some shade. While resting, a Chinese woman came along, bearing a heavy burden. She had brought this burden a number of miles, for which she would receive a small pittance, or what in this country would be so regarded. He stated in his letter that she and her husband had embraced the Christian religion; that her husband had formerly been a butcher, and that for renouncing the religion of their country his customers had all left him; and he had to abandon his business, and was reduced to great straits to make a living. This poor woman had in consequence been compelled to take this long and toilsome walk to make something with which to support life. Elder Simmons' walk, he stated, had been light compared with hers. He thereupon took courage and went on his way. The story was a touching one. I felt I wanted this woman and her husband to know that

one human being, though living on the opposite side
of the globe, had heard their story and had been
moved by it. I thereupon sent Brother Simmons
five dollars to be given her, unless he should know
some reason for not doing so, my meaning being,
unless they had apostatized, which I suppose he understood.

Several months had passed. I had ceased to think
of the little incident, when one day as I lay on my
bed a letter was handed me from Brother Simmons·
He had received the money, and had given it to the
poor woman. They were thankful indeed. The same
envelope contained a letter from the husband and
wife, written to me in Chinese. I regretted that
Brother Simmons had not translated it. In his letter
he told me they had a little girl they wanted to educate in our Canton schools, but they were too poor
to do so. He told me the sum required, but did not
ask me for any help. I determined to aid in her
education, and have done so. This is the way I came
to be interested in this little girl. I have now (January, 1891,) contributed to her education for five
years. In one year more, I learn from Brother Simmons, her education will be completed, and she will
be qualified to teach. Two years ago, the coming
spring, the little girl professed religion and was baptized. This account may at some future day be
interesting to my children.

GREAT CHANGES have taken place in the habits and business methods of the people since I was a boy. Labor-saving machines without number have been invented, greatly multiplied, and brought into use in every department of business. In my earlier days families did not buy the quantity of dry goods they do now. The spinning wheel and loom were then to be found in every family. The white women of the country spun and wove much of the cloth that was used in the family. During the winter months the negro women on the plantations were employed in spinning, and some in weaving. When a boy, I spooled, warped and put in the loom, and through the sley and harness, and wove many a piece of cloth. I was sometimes required to do the ironing for the family; but there were some things I never did: I never washed clothes nor milked a cow.

The wheel for spinning flax was also common. Spinning flax was a beautiful and rapid work. My mother was very fond of it, and was a rapid spinner. All classes were to a large extent clothed with fabrics made at home; and the household was in this way largely supplied with cotton, woolen and flaxen goods.

Tan yards were in every neighborhood. At these the leather was tanned for making shoes, harness, etc. The people lived well and comfortably, and more at-home then than now. There was more general industry, and less running about than at the

present day. My mother did the sewing for a large
white and colored family with the needle. Sewing
machines have come into use long since I was a
grown man.

I can recollect when a few old farmers still used
the reap-hook for cutting wheat and oats; but this
had been very generally abandoned for the scythe
and cradle; and these to a large extent have been
supplanted by the reaper. We then trod out wheat
mainly with horses Since then this practice has
been entirely abandoned for the thresher.

Tobacco and wheat were the leading monied sta-
ples in that part of Virginia where my father lived.
The tobacco was prized in large hogsheads, weighing
from 1800 to 2000 pounds. These were carried to
market on wagons. The wagons usually brought
back dry goods or groceries. Richmond and Farm-
ville were our leading tobacco and wheat markets.

When my father was a young man it was quite
common to roll tobacco to market I have seen
tobacco taken to market in this way. Felloes were
put around the hogshead near each end, and an axle
was fixed to the ends of the hogshead, to which a
frame tongue, or something in the nature of a tongue,
was fixed. A yoke of oxen or two horses would in
this way roll a hogshead very easily. This way of
taking tobacco to market was inclined to damage it,
as it would have to be rolled through the mud, if
any, and the little arbitged streams. Between

were also used on Stanton and Dan rivers, and I
suppose on other streams in the State, for carrying
heavy produce to market. They usually carried
eight or ten hogsheads at a time. They were com-
monly manned by three hands'; one a sternman, and
two to work at the poles in going up stream. They
made good speed, with but little labor, in going down
stream; but in coming up stream the batteau (boat)
had to be poled. This was a hard and laborious
work. They generally had a bugle on board, which
some of the hands would occasionally wind.

For many years after my father came to Tennessee
the cotton, tobacco and wheat was generally hauled from the neighborhood of McLemoresville to
Wills' Point, or to some other place on the Tennessee River. Occasionally some would be hauled to
Hickman, Kentucky. My grandchildren will understand there were no railroads in the country at the
time of which I am now speaking. The telegraph
has been invented and brought into use within my
recollection.

My health gave way in the summer of 1876, since
which time I have been unable to attend to any active business. My two younger children have little,
if any, recollection when their father was in active
life. They recollect me only as a broken-down man.
I little thought, ten or twelve years ago, that I
should live to see all my children grown, but I have
lived to see my youngest son reach manhood. And

more, they are all Christian men and Christian
women.

The Lord has mercifully lengthened out my days.
I desire to be thankful. May my children ever walk
in the light and in the fear of God. May they never
cease to remember that the fear of the Lord is the
beginning of wisdom. May they be useful in their
day and generation, and may the blessing of heaven
ever rest upon them.

www.ingramcontent.com/pod-product-compliance
Lightning Source LLC
Chambersburg PA
CBHW070856280326
41934CB00008B/1466